THE POETRY OF SPACES

SARAH ANDREWS

This book belongs to

. . . .

A guide to creating authentic and beautiful spaces,
that can be used by you, wherever you are. Anywhere and
everywhere – or maybe somewhere one day.

THE POETRY OF SPACES

SARAH ANDREWS

Hardie Grant

BOOKS

'Almost as
if we closed
our eyes and
wished hard
enough for
everything to
be just right,
everything to

be safe and
wonderful ...
and as we
close the door
behind us and
step over
the threshold,
it is so.'

For the White Queen.

Whose daily habit, 'to believe six impossible things before breakfast',
inspired a lifetime of doing the same. So, it is to her that I dedicate this book.

Table of Contents.

INTRODUCTION

Never underestimate the wisdom and complexity of children's books. In CS Lewis's *The Voyage of the Dawn Treader*, the story's heroes meet an old man with a silver beard that reaches the floor on an island at the beginning of Earth's end. He tells them that he is, in fact, a star, tired from his celestial dance up in the sky and has come to this lonely island to rest awhile. One of the children finds it hard to believe that an earthly man could be a star, and blurts out, 'But, Sir, in our land a star is just a huge flaming ball of gas.' To which the star replies, 'My son, even in your world, that is not what a star is, but only what a star is made of.'

We are so often told and shown what our homes *should be*, visually bombarded with perfect white cottages, gleaming marble kitchens, subway tiles, the exact right stack of books on the exact coffee table of the moment/month or year. But my work is about what a home *is*. Home was the first universe we have all ever known, and now, as grown-ups our homes are our own personal cosmoses around us.

In the outside world we can often feel vulnerable, anonymous, overlooked and with no real control over what surrounds us. In our home, we can quite literally lock the door to the external world and step into another dimension. Almost as if we closed our eyes and wished hard enough for everything to be just right, everything to be safe and wonderful … and as we close the door behind us and step over the threshold, it is so. Our spaces are not a static box of geometry and materials, they are living machines of experience, safety, wonder, curation and something far deeper – our inner worlds reflected outer, perhaps.

I think 'curiously restless' might be the best way to describe the way I have lived my life so far. Thinking about it now, I have spent the last 20 years no more than a few months at a time in one place. The one constant has always been the desire to create a lockable refuge from the storm the world can often be.

A royal green sloop named 'Gabrielle', all mahogany, red velvet and vintage cowboy prints that I tried to sail alone around the world in.

My own floating universe where I was Captain Cook and she was my 'Endeavour'. Together sailing into distant bays, so devoid of people I really did feel like I was discovering new lands. The irony is, as a young woman, it was myself I was discovering in the absence of the world telling me what I needed to be.

A childhood sleep-out I moved myself out to part-time as a small child. My parents affectionately called it The Nun's Room, in reference to my attitude to life, preferring to shut myself away alone with a book to the company of all others, including them. The Nun's Room has seen a few iterations over my lifetime. Returning to it and revamping it into the space I needed around me whenever life went astray. Once after a shipwreck (sadly, see above), again after a divorce (unfortunately, see below). The one constant being the lock on the door, the curtains drawn and, an escape from everything that was tormenting me, in the pages of an old encyclopedia I'd found, my favourite of which included folklore and fairytales alongside science and geography. The lust for both fact and fancy has never worn off. I personally feel the two are the same, the latter just not fully understood yet.

A small white cabin perched on the edge of a forest overlooking the inky black inland waters of a wild southern island far, far away – which I named Captains Rest, a world I created for myself when the one I was in, suburban, married, picket white fence, turned unsurprisingly upside down. A true shelter from the storm that plagued my life at that time, and an actual one – living alone cosily by a fireplace observing the world through the enormous antique windows I installed to watch the goings-on around me in their purest forms. Oceans and skies and mountains and forests going about their daily business while the rest of the world has forgotten them. A family of wild ducks I slowly coaxed day by day into becoming good company, a little white rowboat for when I felt the urge to explore a little.

There have been so many more wonderful worlds which I have had the chance to create, not only of my own, but now in a roundabout way, through many thousands of my students and clients around the world. The journey from being a young woman drifting alone at sea to creating work that has brought so much honest good at a time when the world needs it has been an unlikely one. What do they say? Man plans, god laughs? I've always loved that idea, after the adventure that life has been so far, it's the truest thing I know.

In a traditional sense, I was trained as both a spatial scientist, and as a designer. I've always loved arts and sciences, both a language for making sense of our inner and outer worlds. After the enormous but unlikely success of 'far away, in a place no one ever visits' Captains Rest as an Airbnb, I brought the two together to create a series of unique learnings in my Hosting Masterclass for those creating spaces to share. But only after a lot of badgering by so many who wanted to know just what the magic was that I knew. In an instant, all those studying with me were on the covers of magazines world over, too, leading my small community workshops to becoming a fully fledged school teaching thousands and quietly and quickly achieving cult status for all looking to create authentic spaces, be it for themselves or for their businesses.

My first book *Principles of Style* came along next, based on some of the teaching I used to help guide my students, many of whom were stepping nervously into the world of interiors for the first time, and often claiming not to have a creative bone in their bodies. It was so untrue – we are just not taught, and instead are told that basic skills are reserved for a special few who are born with them. Through the 10 principles carefully illustrated in *Principles of Style,* alongside aesthetic experiments showing the nuances of each, I opened my school Principles of Styling & Storytelling, a place for everyone to be guided step by step to create their own authentic spaces, tell their own stories, and find their own way in a world that is otherwise becoming less than individual.

Of all the worlds I've had the chance to create and enjoy over my life, it's this last one – the schools and the communities that they have built – which have been, by far, the most incredible. To create something new, and honest, in this world where selling has taken priority over helping. And to offer something that works, and to demystify what had felt unachievable to almost everyone, started a journey through bedrooms and hallways and ended up shaping entire lives and careers. And futures that our incredible students never thought possible.

And so, all of that has led me to you, dear Reader, reading these words for the first time. What an adventure it has been to get to here. This book offers another small part of my teachings so that you might also be able to step into our world and, if you so choose, one of your own making, too. Five lessons that step out of the principles and into the poetry of our spaces.

The Poetry of Spaces is not about what a home should be made of, it's a guidebook to what it is – a shelter and an incubator for our unique humanness. Five advanced lessons in style gifted from me to you that lift the spaces around you, no matter what they might be, out of the ordinary into the otherworldly. Four whole places, all so wildly different and all so special for you to explore so you can see how each of these elements can be used in unison, and ten rooms from around the world that firmly march to the beat of their own drum, to inspire you that, no matter your taste or place, you can do the same.

So, shall we begin?

PART ONE

5 Lessons in the Foundations of Style

I have been creating and transforming spaces ever since I was a child. Over the years, I have pondered what makes a space feel completely special, otherworldly. I've realised it's not just about its physical aspects – it often has to do with elements that are slightly mysterious and difficult to document. That doesn't mean I can't talk about them, or show them to you – as I have been doing to my students all over the world for the past few years. I'm so happy to be able to share with you five lessons in the foundations of style that I know can help you create a world around you that feels sensitive, beautiful, memorable and completely your own.

Lesson One

LIFE

Have you ever read *A Velveteen Rabbit*? I expect many of you have adored the story about the stuffed toy who becomes more and more loved the shabbier he gets. 'Real isn't how you are made,' said the Skin Horse. 'It's a thing that happens to you.'

The question I always find myself asking looking at house after house is, 'But why is it beautiful?' and the answer so often leads back to there being a sense that a tale has been told here, a life is being truly lived – that this space has been created as a result of a perfectly imperfect human nesting here while our solar system continues its slow spin outside. A little world that is so loved inside a larger one that is mostly out of our control.

When I am putting a space together, it is a real joy to consider life – constructing our spaces as a vessel to hold it and nurture how we want to live rather than how we are told we should. I currently live in The Hermitage. A monastic, mostly empty, largely unfinished home perched on the edge of an island, off an island, tucked in a forest, overlooking the sea. It is here I rest between worldly adventures. The emptiness and unfinishedness is on purpose. I really like wandering around its cavernous space with nothing in it as a reprieve from how overwhelming a busy modern life can be.

My bed is surrounded by piles of books rather than a bedhead or bedside table. I can't seem to happily drift off to sleep unless I've opened a book at random and read a line or two before tucking it lovingly under the pillow I'm sleeping on. No window furnishings exist. I mostly keep the waking hours of 3am until 7pm and, more than any other time of the day, enjoy the dance of the moon sinking over the water and the world waking up all by myself. No real kitchen is discernible, as no real cooking ever gets done here. My bath lives halfway between the sea and my home, to ensure I'm both clean and warmed after an icy morning swim, and that I don't drag too much of the sea and its salt and sand into my home. My lounge room is laid out as a mirror image – a daytime side which looks out to the sea, and a nighttime side facing the fire. Importantly, besides a view and a fire, it holds a cabinet of curiosities where my most precious things live. A kingfisher feather and a sea eagle egg, both found or perhaps gifted to me by this house when I moved in; my first book *Principles of Style* and a ceramic bust my mother gave me, which has fallen off shelves at great heights on more than three documented occasions, but still hasn't broken. I'm convinced it's my current good luck charm.

10

PYGMALION AND GALATEA (C.1890)

I love this painting by Jean-Léon Gérôme, which depicts the story from Ovid's *Metamorphoses* in which the sculptor Pygmalion carves an ivory statue and falls in love with it. After leaving offerings to the goddess Aphrodite, he returns home and kisses his statue, only to find her lips warm and his wish come true – she had been brought to life. The studio itself is so full of life, too.

11

SIDNEY HALL'S ASTRONOMICAL CHART

This illustration of the constellations Leo Major and Leo Minor was first published in 1831. Across the cultures for thousands of years, humans have tried to use what they know, or are familiar with, as a way of explaining the unknown. The stars in the night sky are a vehicle, in a number of different forms, to relate mythical stories, describe experiences and portray belief systems.

I shudder to think how anyone else could possibly live here, but there is nowhere else in the world I am more content than in this perfect world built just for me. As Ilse Crawford puts it, it's my 'frame for life'. And, exploring so many others' 'frames' and continually asking myself, 'Why is it beautiful?', it's always a sense of life, of realness in them that moves me so deeply. Almost as if the clues scattered around feel like an orchestra of hidden imperfection that together write such a lovely symphony. After all, it's the very definition of uniqueness that is imperfection.

I dare you, pick up a stack of magazines now and flick through. Be curious about those spaces that capture both your heart and your imagination – we're all human and, whether we're always aware of it or not, connect to the humanness innately around us. Perhaps an attempt has been made with the standard bowl of lemons added to the gleaming white kitchen, or a perfectly tonal stack of three beige books put on a coffee table, which is sitting in the pin straight living room – but the spaces that excite me the most invite me into another life, another world, so that I may try it on and see what it might be all about. This chapter explores them.

Loving *The Velveteen Rabbit* as much as I did may be the reason I have always gravitated towards the slightly overlooked and unloved, the less than perfect but always with a tale to tell. Or maybe it's the other way round – maybe *The Velveteen Rabbit* is a story that we all understand intrinsically, in our bones, without even realising it. 'Generally, by the time you are Real, most of your hair has been loved off, and your eyes drop out and you get loose in the joints and very shabby. But these things don't matter at all, because once you are Real you can't be ugly, except to people who don't understand.'

CHRISTINE'S VACATION HOUSE, NORWAY

Opposite & pages 14–15 This lovely house has been in interior designer Christine's family for more than 400 years. She has found balance between honouring the home's history with her own interests.

A lover of colour and of sustainability, Christine has filled it with secondhand finds that are given new life in their new surroundings. This is definitely a home with a past and a present.

16

EXPERIMENT 1:

Let's look at a simple home vignette you often see. A bed, a bedside table and some
flowers. Everything in its right place. Ironed, straightened, the clutter of life put away.
Lovely, but to me it feels empty – something is missing.

17

Experiment 2:

And now let's let some life in here. Signs that this space is being used – maybe flowers
have been collected on a walk rather than bought, pre-arranged, from a store.
To me, this is the space I want to linger in.

SARAH & ADAM'S CHURCH, WILLUNGA, AUSTRALIA

Page 18 A friend of mine's home that, in summary, is an ode to things that express her deepest joy. Both in her things, and in her people, big and small. I think one of the main lessons here in bringing life into a space is to not try and make everything match or be too perfect – I love it that there's a mixture of pots for the indoor plants and that the furniture looks lived-in.

HÔTEL DRUJON, VALLABRÈGUES, FRANCE

Page 19, opposite & above, pages 22–23 Atelier Vime is a wicker and rattan workshop based in an 18th-century hôtel. For longer than anyone can trace, wickerwork has been the main trade in the area, which the owners have celebrated in the restoration of this building. Again, there's a lot that doesn't match and signs of life are emphasised rather than being hidden away.

24

HÔTEL DRUJON, VALLABRÈGUES, FRANCE

This bathroom says such a lot about Benoît Rauzy and Anthony Watson, the founders of Atelier Vime, and their sense of design and life. The herringbone tiles that hold echoes of weaving and the handmade; the mural which doesn't take itself too seriously and adds a touch of whimsy to the room. A bathroom needs to be functional, but that doesn't mean it can't have personality.

25

CAROLE POIROT'S HOME, NORTH YORKSHIRE, UK

What I really love about this bedroom of photographer Carole Poirot is that it gives you such a lovely sense of who she is and her work as an artist. There's a subtlety to everything she does and that comes through so clearly in the way she has put her home together – the soft colour of the walls, the arrangement on the shelves, even the way she has hung the overhead light.

DORRAINA HOUSE, SWITZERLAND

Pages 26–27 & above A historic building, originally a farmhouse for people and animals, and now used as a vacation home for Mierta Casty, daughter of artist Gian Casty. The murals are by Gian Casty, and help to give the place so much character and individuality. They're obviously incredibly precious to the family, and so vibrant that little else is needed in the space.

29

THE HERMITAGE, TASMANIA, AUSTRALIA

How we live is our own responsibility. My pantry contains the items I use a lot – cups, plates, saucers, along with the talismans of my life I like to see a lot. Gifts from the wild beach outside, a bust given to me by my mother and ceramic gifts made by a student who is an artist. Surrounding yourself only with things that mean something to you help present such a clear picture of who you are.

30

NOVECENTO, VENICE, ITALY

Gioele and his wife Heiby opened Novecento in 2002 with the aim of offering visitors not just a room, but rather an authentic experience of the city and its people. Focusing on your immediate surroundings, whatever and wherever they may be, and celebrating them, can be the best way to create an environment that's authentic, unforgettable and life enhancing.

31

NOVECENTO, VENICE, ITALY

To me, this room has enormous character and life, and a subtlety to the way it is handled. I love the combination of elements – the different styles of timber furniture, comfortable but slightly austere, the extravagance of the curtains, the traditional terrazzo floor. It's all been put together with such care, but there's also an ease to it that I find really appealing.

32

ODILE BOUSCARAT, PROVENCE, FRANCE

I recently had the pleasure of meeting Odile. She was born in Paris, but has spent the past 30 years in Provence. She's a collector of 18th century textiles, objects and wallpapers, which she restores, repairs and showcases for the next generation. Her store, La Petite Curieuse, is tucked away in a little alleyway in L'Isle sur la Sorgue, away from other antique shops, and is open by appointment only.

ODILE BOUSCARAT, PROVENCE, FRANCE

The experience of meeting Odile and hunting through selected stacks of precious old fabrics allowed me to enter the world of the artists, printmakers and textile artisans who designed and created them often centuries ago. I've now started collecting antique fabrics and papers, and spend many hours wondering about the overlooked and forgotten artists who made them.

Lesson Two

LIGHT

Light, and its constant companion, shadow. Two eternal lovers that bring the otherworldly to a room, but always the first that are missed. Maybe because they're ephemeral and elusive, they are often left off lists that feature paint, lamps and sofas. But, deal with them as a practical afterthought at your peril; without their mesmerising dance, your spaces will always fall flat.

Before we even start thinking about the effect light and shadow can have on your immediate surroundings, and talk about how to handle them, let's look at the wider world. There's a line in *Lust for Life*, Irving Stone's fictionalised version of van Gogh's life, that says, 'The one who has not seen Paris in the morning does not know how beautiful it is'. I take that to mean the really early morning, just as the city is coming back to life, with soft sunlight on the stonework and long shadows on the cobblestones. The same place at midday, or on a cloudy day, in springtime or summer, in the early evening or late at night – the atmosphere each time is totally different, and a lot of that has to do with light and shadow. Which time is the best is ultimately a matter of taste – each is lovely in its own way.

The same can be said for anywhere, city or not. The sun slowly rising as I look out of my window at dawn, shadows gradually creeping across the grasses and rocks, the soft morning light, the summer midday sun bleaching colour from the scene … you see what I mean.

Hopefully now you get the idea that light and shadow are intrinsic to life – marking moments in time, transporting us, changing the way we feel. In an extreme example, Meursault, the narrator of Albert Camus' *The Stranger*, stuck in a prison cell, contemplates his mother's belief that, no matter how miserable you are, there's always something to be thankful for. Every morning as sunlight flooded that desperate place, he knew she was right.

Look at the way theatre lighting designers play with light and shadow, creating different moods and effects with each – or talk to any good photographer, and they'll tell you they're a painter with light, which is such a powerful way of looking at things, and should give you some idea of what a difference they can make.

THE GREAT COMET of 1881.

Observed on the Night of June 25–26 at 1h 30m A.M.

THE GREAT COMET OF 1881 FROM THE TROUVELOT ASTRONOMICAL DRAWINGS (1881–1882)

I find this astronomical drawing by E.L. Trouvelot so moving, with the points of manmade light against something bolder and more dramatic. Light is what allows us to experience reality and interpret beauty. Without it, the world would be a colourless mass, and most things would struggle to survive. In its absence, the appearance of it is otherworldly. A starry night, a shooting star, a fireplace.

sous L'AILE D'OMBRE l'être noir appliquait une active morsure.........

37

IN THE SHADOW OF THE WING, THE BLACK CREATURE BIT (1891)

I love it that the word 'light', which in one form or another can be found in many ancient languages, refers to so much more than the light we see. In fact, 'seeing the light' is more about knowledge than anything visual. Pythagoras believed that the eye was a lighthouse for our souls, which is such a beautiful image. Light, and shadow, can be seen so clearly in this work by Odilon Redon.

No one understands lighting more or, more to the point, the importance of shadows, I think, than the Japanese. In Jun'ichirō Tanizaki's beautiful essay on aesthetics, *In Praise of Shadows*, he talks about the roof of a Japanese house being the first thing to be considered – something to throw a shadow on the earth. It's in the pale light of the shadow that the rest of the house comes together. Isn't that just the most delicate and delightful thought? The roof of a Western house, he believes, is there to keep out wind and rain, and built to create as few shadows as possible. On every page there's at least one absolutely amazing insight – the fact that Westerners can look at a Japanese room, and think it looks very plain, whereas its true beauty comes from a variety of shadows – light and heavy – layered over each other. Or that Japanese lacquerware looks its best in the half-light.

Before I start to consider almost anything else, I think about light. How much do I want in order to create the feeling I'm after. In general, for me, as much as possible, but there are areas, such as bedrooms, where shadows are more important to me. I think about where I can add windows, where I can put glass in doors, where – failing that – a mirror could go. I try to avoid window dressings, except where they're absolutely necessary for privacy reasons or to block out any harsh direct sunlight. I totally understand what the American architect Louis Kahn meant when he said, 'The sun never knew how great it was until it hit the side of a building.'

Once I have designed my space and worked out how natural light – and shadows – will work within it, I'll start thinking about artificial light. My personal philosophy is to hang lighting low, on the wall as a sconce, or to use lamps and, occasionally, candles. I never ever use lighting on, or in, the ceiling – it does nothing to add to the atmosphere. Pendant lights, hung much lower than expected, are another matter. It's so much better, too, to use far less light than you think you'll need – the effect is so powerful and creates an absolute dreamscape during those hours when the sun is somewhere else in the world.

Light can come from unexpected sources. Tanizaki talks of Westerners loving glittery, shiny things – and polishing knives and forks until they're glinting. Japanese people, on the other hand, would rather leave their kettles and sake cups alone, and enjoy them best when they take on a smoky patina. If you're trying to create as much light as possible, gleaming objects can help; for more shadowy spaces, forget about polishing.

CAPTAINS REST, TASMANIA, AUSTRALIA

Opposite & pages 40–41 The installation of a wall of antique glass windows, reflecting the light bouncing off the sea and refracting into the space, gives a constantly shifting dream-like quality to the experience of being inside my Tasmanian cabin. With privacy not an issue, I have no need for window dressings, and love watching the play of shadows across the space.

42

EXPERIMENT 1:

Daylight The qualities of light we have available to us are often missed.
These experiments show their effect on the poetry of space.
My preference has always been for soft daylight.

43

EXPERIMENT 2:

Candlelight A close second. I find it interesting that the two light sources
that come from the natural world – the sun and its earthly cousin,
fire – cast the most soothing glaze over our lives and space.

44

EXPERIMENT 3:

Lamplight We are lucky enough to be able to make light when it's naturally not
available to us. I find that shading bulbs, and forcing the light downwards so it's soft
on the eye, to be the most pleasing and gentle in dark spaces.

45

EXPERIMENT 4:

Overhead light Notice how harsh artificial direct light can be? I try to use
as little as possible, and attempt to shade or direct it downwards so it can softly
bounce where needed. Never be afraid of a little darkness.

TOWNHOUSE BY RETROUVIUS, LONDON, UK

Daylight streaming in from one side always looks best. From the one direction, each object and part of the room is highlighted in both light and shade, giving spaces contrast. Retrouvius, a company that salvages materials and then uses them in the interiors they design, has panelled the bed nook in this London townhouse in reclaimed cheese boards, which is one of their longstanding specialities.

TOWNHOUSE BY RETROUVIUS, LONDON, UK

Above & pages 48–49 Lime wash and lime plaster are two of my very favourite wall treatments. Lime has a high index of refraction, which means it can bend light like a prism. As light shifts through the day and night, the walls give an ever-changing glow, which can never be the case with paint. A rescued 17th century fireplace introduces even more lovely texture into the sitting room of a Georgian townhouse.

52

SUMMER RESIDENCE, KATTEGAT, DENMARK

Pages 50–51, above & opposite Light is so precious to the Scandinavians, which is not surprising, given the long dark winters they face every year. In this summer residence, none of the surfaces absorb light – instead they celebrate it and let it bounce around. At night under lamplight or candlelight, the rooms take on a different character – mesmerising and intensely atmospheric.

MERCHANT'S HOUSE, HASTINGS, UK

Pages 54–57 Alastair Hendy describes the restoration of his Tudor house as 'putting back the years the years have taken away', as it had been made quite contemporary when he bought it. It's an ode to time, craftsmanship and history, but also to shadows. A celebration of how beautiful light is, but also the magic of the dark – and the poetry those two make when they play together.

58

EELKE JAN BLES'S HOUSE, AUVERGNE, FRANCE

In Dutch designer Eelke Jan Bles's house in the Auvergne, light bounces off the perfectly aged walls, and the simple styling helps highlight the beauty of the space. There are ways of soothing the mistakes of a badly lit room – but, similarly, distracting, busy styling can dull the magic of one that is lit perfectly. Lighting is one of the most powerful tools we have access to, but is often underestimated.

59

The Bowmont, Tasmania, Australia

Tasmania is full of heritage buildings, one of which is The Bowmont, housed in a former bank which was once also a hospital. This photo reminds me to tell you a trick about side lighting of a room, which is always the most beautiful. If you are photographing a space with light coming in from more than one direction, control it by closing blinds or doors, or having someone hold a blanket up.

60

PALAZZO DANIELE, SALENTO, ITALY

Above & opposite The monastic decor in the exaggerated grandeur of this hotel works so sublimely due to the masterful play of light and shadow which, in themselves, are elements that fill the halls and rooms. The use of artificial light has been handled so cleverly here – nothing is hidden, everything is surprisingly unadorned, which only helps emphasise the beauty of the spaces.

61

PALAZZO DANIELE, SALENTO, ITALY

Pages 62–63 There's a calm throughout, but also a focus on the unexpected, a very good example of which can be found in the way paintings are lit. Of course, the usual thing to do is to light them discreetly from above. The minimal cylindrical lamp, with its visible cord, throws the most fantastic beam of light onto the painting, creating dramatic shadows and picking up highlights on the gilded frame.

Lesson Three

INSTRUMENTS

Very simply, our homes are made up of four walls, a roof and a collection of objects inside of them. Everyone seems to rush around in a great panic as if all the variations of chairs, tables and lamps are important, so much so that they miss the point that our spaces and our belongings are tools to help us live well. It is here we should slow down and start – rather than jumping ahead to consider the aesthetics of linen vs velvet in a room design, let's say.

Unexpectedly becoming a teacher has been by far the greatest adventure of my life. It has given me the chance to get to know so many of you quite intimately. How you live, what brings you joy, or pain. What it is you really wish for. I get a unique view of your journeys, and how closely they mirror one another. How alike we all really are.

For me, what brings me the most sadness is how my students arrive at my school. Flustered and apologetic that they haven't been able to keep up with the latest interior trend, whatever it might be for the season or the year, frightened that their space isn't beautiful enough for them to be studying with me and adamant that they have no creative talent at all. The sheer amount of visual and aesthetic information delivered to us via social media, pinterest, magazines, in part, is incredible. In another sense, though, seeing, and being told how things should be really is creating a landscape of monoculture in our homes, and a sense of elitism in what should be joyous and available for all to explore wholeheartedly as individuals. Trend forecasters work with big interior companies to help them update their collections, colours and products every six months! Who can keep up? And why should we? Trends are created by those trying to sell you as much as possible, with constant messaging that you need to buy more and update. This is for their benefit, not yours.

We slow our students down, and we ask them to start with themselves – and gradually step them through the art and science of our work. I am pleased to report they leave with a spring in their step and have gone on to not only create the most incredible homes and spaces no matter the budget, but today, opening social media or magazines the world over, I see their work, giving permission for others to explore what it truly is that is beautiful and important to surround themselves with. As a community, they are starting their own trends – timeless interiors based in authenticity, purpose and delight. It is incredible to see just how powerful we are.

MRS BEETON'S BOOK OF HOUSEHOLD MANAGEMENT

First published in 1861, this guide to running a household contains some advice on table setting still current today, keeping in mind its use to facilitate conversation. Some recipes, though, give the impression that Mrs Beeton was not much of a cook, such as instructions to boil pasta for nearly two hours, and a recipe for a toast sandwich of two slices of bread around a buttered slice of toast.

67

BILLETHEAD (C. 1939)

As a sailor, designer and lover of stories, I find this work by Betty Fuerst almost irresistible, combining so many of the things I'm passionate about. Billetheads are carved decorative scrolls used instead of figures at ships' bows. In the age of wooden sailing ships, each vessel was unique and these touches were works of art in themselves, carefully created and holding great meaning.

In our classes, before we broach the aesthetics of furniture and the objects in our spaces, a key idea we teach is to start to think about our objects as instruments to help us live in the way we want to.

To give you an example, clearly I love to read – and I love to spend evenings with a book. So, let's think about that for a minute, and it's obvious to me that I will want the perfect chair – it can't be too hard, because I want to sit in it for hours on end. On the other hand, it can't be too soft and comfortable, otherwise I'll just fall asleep. I'd rather have a single chair than a sofa, but I want to be able to put my feet up somehow.

What's next? I'll obviously need some sort of light. As you might already know, I don't use overhead ceiling lights, so that wouldn't work. I'd prefer something that hangs low and has a soft glow, nothing too bright. And then, there's nothing nicer than having a cup of tea while I'm reading, so I'll need somewhere for that as well as for my stack of books – and I'd like my library to be close by. Where am I imagining myself sitting? Facing out to the water, or in a dark and secluded room? Or perhaps in the sweet surroundings of my bedroom?

Do you see where I'm going with this? With every decision we make when we're putting a room together, we're designing an experience. Or, as I like to put it, using our objects as instruments to help us live well. Rather than thinking about a chair as a chair, we're thinking of how it can be used, how it can make people feel, how it can influence their behaviour.

One of my first loves is creating spaces for people to holiday in. Ultimately, it's my goal to create homes so wonderful, mysterious, comfortable and all-consuming in the best way that they act like medicine to the senses of a world-weary soul. I start building these spaces by considering first the experience I want my guests to have in each moment in my homes, and then use tables, chairs, lighting – that long list of homewares – to build it, almost in a sense creating the experience far before one ever steps into it. Using our objects like a paintbrush, where life comes first, not the look.

Every sofa might be somewhere to sit, but some are best to read on, to dream, to imagine, to feel perfectly content with the world. Others are built for conversation, or perhaps best for a waiting room. The correlation between our surroundings and how we feel is undeniable. They dictate our course in life and, once we understand our homes and our rooms, we develop the power to create spaces that help us live the lives we want for ourselves. Whenever I get the extraordinary opportunity to create a new space, a brand new world to help shape my life, I think of the sage advice from Pablo Picasso, who said, 'I paint objects as I think them, not as I see them.'

My inner desires for my life are the paintbrush, the house, my canvas – and that long list of tables, chairs and lamps, the paint I used to make my world real.

GIL BONGIORNO'S HOUSE, PAVIA, ITALY

The exquisite selection of objects and furniture contained in Gil's house, parts of which date back to around 1250, bring almost a gallery-like appreciation to its things. There's such an art to placement. I always try for triangles when grouping objects, and aim for three layers, which is exactly what you see here. Visual rules give us guidance as a place to start.

70

EXPERIMENT 1:

Let's take a look at chairs. Every chair has its purpose. Maybe these are suited
to a small spot to sit for a cup of tea, a bite to eat. A busy cafe working to move
people on after a meal rather than encourage one to linger.

71

EXPERIMENT 2:

Perhaps something larger, softer might have a purpose in a venue encouraging its
patrons to stick around. A wine bar, jazz club. A library conducive to sitting and
reading. A shift towards objects as aids, rather than a look, helps us live well.

GIL BONGIORNO'S HOUSE, PAVIA, ITALY

Pages 72–73 When we approach our spaces from a place of thinking about who we are, what we will do in various rooms and ponder how we would like to feel when we're in there, they almost take the shape of a poem, an ode to who we are and our dream of living well. For each of us, this will look different, but that's to be celebrated. Gil, a lover of art and fashion, has an innate sense of design.

75

BAYODE ODUWOLE & CLAIRE PRINGLE'S HOUSE, MARGATE, UK

Opposite & above, pages 76–77 Bayode Oduwole and Claire Pringle, founders of the fashion label Pokit, left London to settle in this Georgian house in Margate, on the Kent coast. They see this space as an evolving gallery where they test various layouts, and experiment with different living and working spaces. I love the way they have restored some surfaces while leaving others quite raw.

CREMORNE COTTAGE, SYDNEY, AUSTRALIA

Above & opposite This two-bedroom house, completed in 2022 by AP Design House, is a serene space with a feeling of grandeur that somehow defies its modest size. I'm a huge fan of the work of interior designer Alexandra Ponting, and here she has completed such an artful renovation in which every space and object has purpose, beauty and place. It really is somewhere I would like to linger.

79

CREMORNE COTTAGE, SYDNEY, AUSTRALIA

Pages 80–81 Small spaces can be incredibly challenging to design. The difficulty is in making them functional yet, at the same time, balanced, so as not to be either overwhelming or underwhelming. I like to start with a 50:50 ratio of furniture and objects, and adjust up or down depending on whether I'm trying to create coziness or a sense of calm. It can often take time to get it right.

CREMORNE COTTAGE, SYDNEY, AUSTRALIA

Above & opposite Alexandra Ponting has worked with a mix of original and new features in the renovation, as well as a blend of vintage, custom and contemporary pieces to create a unique and charming space. The balance of objects here helps create the feeling of calm – even though there are many moments of beauty, there are plenty of opportunities for the eye to rest along the way.

EMMA JOHANSSON'S HOUSE, ÄLVSJÖ, SWEDEN

Pages 84–87 The home of writer, photographer and influencer Emma Johansson, built more than 100 years ago, is such a magical mix of patterns and colours. Emma's goal in putting her space together was to make a home filled with creativity and that feels alive. She wanted it to be both practical and beautiful; there's both a warmth and a boldness to it that is very appealing.

88

GIL BONGIORNO'S HOUSE, PAVIA, ITALY

Above & opposite I wanted to show you this house, the oldest part of which was once a convent, to demonstrate the unexpected way objects have been brought together. Part of the strength of the interior lies in the fact that it has been handled so subtly, with some areas restored, while others show the patina of age. This creates a wonderful backdrop for the owner's eclectic collection.

89

THE LANDSCAPE LODGE, ABONDANCE, FRANCE

Pages 90–91 A dear student of mine, Fran, created this space with rest and retreat in mind – it's a place to come back to after a day exploring the mountains, lakes and fields that surround it. There's a softness and warmth to the furniture – it's clearly made for comfort. The lodge is also a celebration of the French Alps, where it is situated, and done in a charming way without any hint of kitsch.

92

NO. 33, BONNIEUX, FRANCE

Above & opposite When nutritionist and food
stylist Rachel Baker was restoring her 13th century
house in the Luberon, she was determined to keep
as much of its original character as possible, which
she has done beautifully. It's furnished simply, with
pre-loved and antique pieces from the area.
There's an authenticity to it that perfectly aligns with
Rachel's approach to health and wellbeing.

93

CONVERTED CONVENT, PIACENZA, ITALY

Pages 94–95 I've always loved reading and, to me, a house without books doesn't feel quite lived-in. The books that we have around us give such an indication of who we are and what we're thinking about. The way the papers are arranged in the open shelves creates a really pleasing scene – with plenty of empty space, there's a balance to them, giving an unexpected sense of calm.

96

PALAZZO, TUSCANY, ITALY

Once home to a noble family, this palazzo had been abandoned for several years before being restored by architect Sabrina Bignami. One of the things I particularly love is how things from different times and places sit happily together. Frescoes by Tuscan painter Luigi Catani, uncovered during the works, now provide an unexpected backdrop for the much less ornate mid-century furniture.

97

PALAZZO, TUSCANY, ITALY

The kitchen is one room in which Sabrina Bignami's confidence in combining pieces from different eras and different places shines through so well. With such a beautiful building, it could be tempting to use only centuries-old antiques, but this would probably make it feel more like a museum. Introducing such a broad range of furniture, lighting and decorative pieces brings new life to the palazzo.

Lesson Four

MATERIALS

I have a personal hypothesis that almost everything we do in an attempt at beauty and comfort in our homes is actually a hunger to bring us back to nature – where we lived, not too long ago. Think about it. We toy with advancing lighting in its natural and manmade forms; we get it just right when it resembles light leaking through the canopy of a redwood forest just barely kissing the soft mossy floor. We obsess online – and it reflects in our pockets – over indoor plants, gardens where we are lucky enough to have them, food and cooking. Oh, and our beloved pets – the wilder of the common pair, the house cat, has half of the entire internet dedicated to it. Show me a more beautiful wall than one made of glass, add a few million on to that home if the world outside all that glass is the ocean, or the forest or the mountains. Please let me know if you have all three of these, I'd like to come visit.

We are made of atoms, the same stuff as the stars. And so I'm not surprised we'd want to surround ourselves with what we came from in our lifelong attempts to find meaning. We share 35 per cent of our DNA with a daffodil, 50 per cent with a tree. Interestingly we also share slightly more of what we are made of with cats than dogs – 8 per cent more for those who are wondering.

I feel like science has always just helped make sense of what we, the poets, artists and dreamers have always known. Astronomers have recently shown that about half the atoms in our bodies were originally formed far beyond our home, the solar system, reaching us on intergalactic winds formed by giant exploding stars. We really are made from stars, travelling from one place to the next, born old souls, scientists think somewhere in the realm of 14 billion years old.

After putting our place in the universe into context – where we came from, how old we are and how closely we are related to a flower – I hope this lesson on materials comes into focus for you. Think about walking barefoot over a grassy meadow on a warm day. How about over a well-worn oak floor. What about over a silk rug? Tile? Vinyl? Try to order these experiences in your head in terms of how much pleasure they give you.

The more closely related to the materials around us we are, or – perhaps the easiest way to think of it is – the more closely related to nature they are, the more pleasure they bring us.

FEMALE – THIRTEEN DRAPERY STUDIES (1868)

Sir Edward Burne-Jones was a British painter, illustrator and designer, who was a founding partner in the designer William Morris's company. I've chosen to show this as I've always particularly loved this study of form in drapery. His paintings reflect romantic dreams, with picturesque scenes of how one would want things to be, a vision I align with when it comes to home.

Our five senses – sight, touch, smell, taste, hearing – communicate our external world into a series of visual images in our brain. It's not our eyes that 'see', it's the orchestra of all of these senses we use constantly that build an image inside ourselves, our consciousness. It's this image that triggers our feelings. Our feelings start a dialogue with our body and our nervous systems.

We are a constant miraculous symphony of consciousness, and our bodies are a tuned instrument of feeling. We recognise quality and materiality without really needing to tell ourselves to do so. Materials that come straight from nature, such as silk, cotton, wool, stone, wood, linen, make us feel comfortable, happy – home. As Alexandra Stoddard, an American designer and pioneer of the happiness movement, puts it, 'If we have authentic, honest, earthy materials in our houses, we'll be more authentic, honest and natural.'

She's right – I think she'd agree with me that there's nothing that takes us out of home and puts us straight back into the screechiness of a chaotic harsh modern world than things like extension cords, the TV remote and polyester tags. But imagine a spot where you sit and read, comfortable armchair covered in soft linen, hand-knitted blanket over an arm, a lampshade on cotton flex hanging from a hook in the ceiling, your feet burrowed into that sheepskin on the floor. Fingers holding soft paper.

When you're thinking about materials, first consider those which come from plants or the ground. Trees not only produce wood, but cork, rattan, bamboo, paper. Plants produce natural fibres such as linen, wool, cotton, flax and jute. From stone we can use granite, marble, sandstone, slate – and sand, which produces glass. Metals such as iron, copper, tin and silver are so beautiful to touch and use, and from the earth itself we can make bricks and terracottas.

There are ethical ways to use materials originating from animals – you can buy cruelty free wool and silk, but my favourite has always been to buy secondhand or antique furs, silks, leather, alpaca, mohair and cashmere. In a sense, I've always felt like it's a sort of rescue, giving them a new life and honouring the animal they came from.

Each one of these natural forms around us provide softness, security, protection, warmth, pleasure. The atoms of materials we choose to surround ourselves with are like tuning forks for our bodies, which are brilliant complex machines of feeling and thinking – made of ancient stardust, travelling from one galaxy to the next.

AUKE DIJKSTRA'S PFARRHAUS RECKNITZ, MECKLENBURG, GERMANY

I am particularly interested in how light moves through natural materials such as lime, wood, stone and linen. When light hits a surface, it passes through, scatters or is reflected in various ways to create our visual world. If you notice how light hits walls painted with plastic paints, it can be harshly reflected rather than softly scattered. There is more science in art than we first realise!

104

EXPERIMENT 1:

An experiment that differs this time. There is no right or wrong way, or wrong
choices to be made here – the materials we select help us tell a story. More formal,
manmade and designed items here speak to an urban, architectural story.

105

EXPERIMENT 2:

In our second take, we've chosen items that are found, torn, minimally processed.
When combined, they tell a simple story of comfort that's both relaxed and humble.
Materials have such a powerful tale to tell.

108

AUKE DIJKSTRA'S PFARRHAUS RECKNITZ, MECKLENBURG, GERMANY

Pages 106–07 Materials can help tell our story, and enrich our senses. Leather, metal, wood without the softness of a rug or cushion all speak to masculinity, consideration, contemplation. Imagine how different this room would feel to us if the chairs were swapped with soft sofas, wool blankets over their arms. I'm not saying it would look better, it would just be another room entirely.

109

HOLIDAY HOME, MALLORCA, SPAIN

Opposite & above This recently renovated historic home, perched upon a hilltop, is a masterclass in materiality. Each element has been chosen with such deep meaning and it translates. A ceiling and floors of Scottish oak from its owner's homeland; bed, collected and earnestly treasured, and eventually finding its way here; stone from the rocky outcrops that protect the house.

110

CHÂTEAU DE LA CARRIÈRE, LOIRE VALLEY, FRANCE

Above & opposite It has been such a pleasure meeting and teaching Suzi, the Australian owner of this incredible château in the Loire Valley. She has spent years gently restoring this historic place and, because many of its original features had been stripped away, filling it with a wonderful mix of treasures and objects that enrich the owner's, and her guests', senses.

WOOLLAHRA HOUSE, SYDNEY, AUSTRALIA

Pages 112–13 The two-storey former gallery and auction house was renovated by AP Design House, with a focus on an appreciation for its Art Deco origins and a sophisticated European air.

Materiality here contributes to a beautiful pairing of softness and strength, which can be seen in the combination of such things as stone and linen, bentwood and steel.

114

WOOLLAHRA HOUSE, SYDNEY, AUSTRALIA

Above & opposite Designer Alexandra Ponting chose to use tadelakt, a Moroccan finish, and travertine in the bathroom. The term tadelakt, meaning 'to rub in', is created when nearly finished lime plaster is polished with a stone to make it water repellent. This lovely material has such a soft, undulating character, and is very organic in form, yet is so clearly the work of a master craftsperson.

115

AUKE DIJKSTRA'S PFARRHAUS RECKNITZ, MECKLENBURG, GERMANY

Pages 116–17 The experiments in this chapter show that our choice of materials influences how spaces make us feel. Homes and spaces can be considered as machines to shape our experience. In our school, we encourage students to ask what a space needs to give to its occupants first, and find materials that work towards that. It's interesting to think about what this space could give to the people who live there.

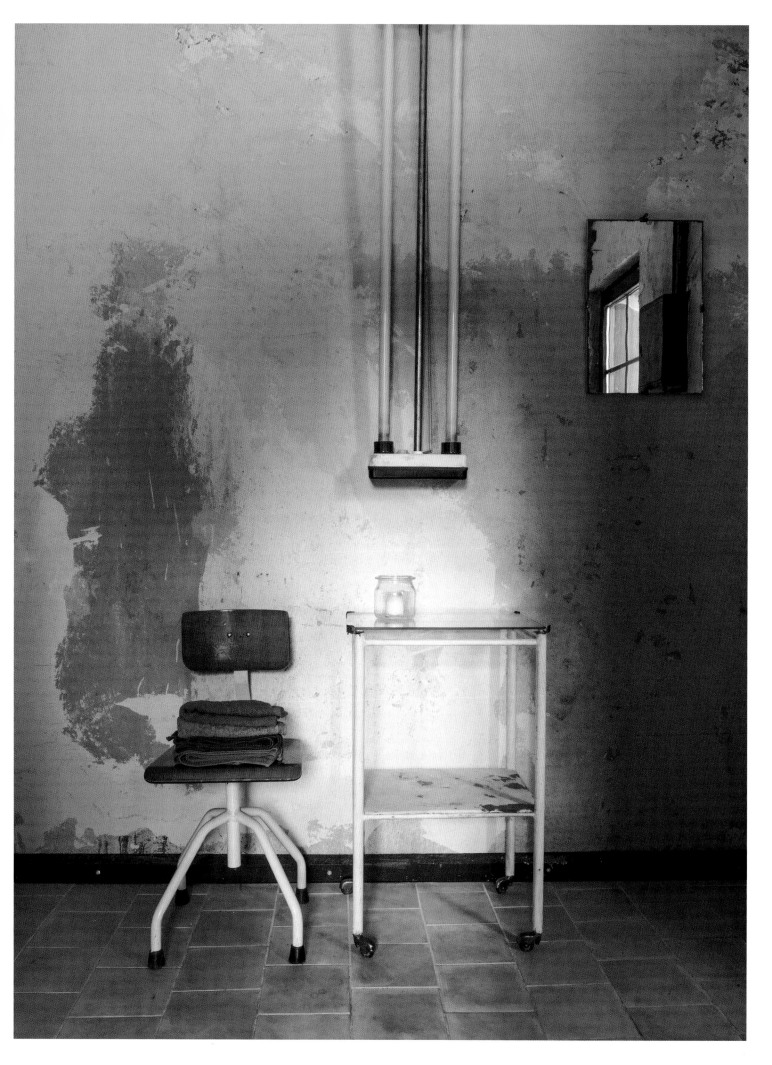

118

THE COLD PRESS, LONDON, ENGLAND

A gallery within an old townhouse in Spitalfields, which also includes a studio and an artist's residence, exhibits emerging and established artists who use natural materials and have a focus on process and craftsmanship. What I really like about the spaces, which are unadorned, authentic and show the passage of time, is that they reflect the intention of the gallery and its artists.

119

ATELIER ELLIS, ENGLAND

Atelier Ellis is a natural paint company founded by colourist Cassandra Ellis. 'I research and craft colours that feel human – complex and deep, but also quiet and cocooning,' she says. I really like her philosophy of designing colours that form a framework for creating the stories that place the occupants at the centre of their homes – that's so much how I think homes should be.

PREDRAG PAJDIC'S HOUSE, SAINT-HIPPOLYTE-DU-FORT, FRANCE

Above & opposite When the artist, art historian and curator restored his house in the South of France, he preserved its original features, which are highlighted by the use of white throughout. Colour psychology is incredibly interesting, as it helps us marry colour and purpose in a space. White is a good choice if you want to create a space that feels like a blank page of a notebook waiting to be written upon.

121

MARSTON HOUSE, PROVENCE, FRANCE

Pages 122–25 Paul and Sharon of Marston House divide their time between the States and Provence. Paul has an architectural practice and Sharon has an antiques business – together they have a number of rental properties, one of which you can see here. What's really special about their places is that they look as if they have evolved over time, with elements added gradually.

MARSTON HOUSE, PROVENCE, FRANCE

Above & opposite Spaces are built to be inhabited, and bathrooms often get overlooked in this regard. More care needs to be taken with styling because of the presence of water; however, artwork, washable rugs and wooden furniture can all live happily in such an environment. When you're planning a space, it's good to focus on the unexpected, which the owners of Marston House do so well.

127

APARTMENT, OSLO, NORWAY

Pages 128–29 We live in the age of aesthetic superiority over the other senses. Materials in a space need to help rather than hinder us. Our bedrooms are our nests – for sleeping, reading, binge watching, recovering from illness, tending to grief, and so many other things. It's the small intimate details that can add depth to our lives and address our emotional needs.

130

MONTPELIER HOUSE, HAY-ON-WYE, UK

Above & opposite Val Harris, who owns two art galleries, spent a year restoring a former bookshop, retaining the lime plaster, wherever possible, and using a neutral palette as a backdrop to her extensive art collection. Older homes such as this one retain a lived-in beauty that can't be artificially created. The lime captures the story of the building, and only gets better over time.

131

MONTPELIER HOUSE, HAY-ON-WYE, UK

Pages 132–35 As well as lime used on the walls, another element in this house that truly indicates the passage of time is the flooring. The imperfections in the surface are not erased; in the hallway, signs where a carpet runner was once laid are clearly visible. A chaise is far from perfect as well – to me, this is a house that feels so lived in, loved and welcoming.

Lesson Five

SENSE

The most compelling spaces I have experienced have left me feeling like my soul was slowly expanding. If space commands all of our five senses – rather than just the forerunners, sight and touch – a richness of otherness occurs that I've always felt difficult to put into words. There is something medicinal about this cross-sensory pollination that is so often left out of our interior considerations.

Science historian and poet, Diane Ackerman (a woman after my own heart) has written a book that everyone must read at least once. In *A Natural History of the Senses*, she explores the biological machinery behind each of our senses – and how we use them to explore the edges of our consciousness. She says, 'Nothing is more memorable than a scent' – the way our brains work means that we don't have to consciously think about what particular smells mean to us.

Scent is essentially liquid memory, and the key to helping create an experience that truly transports. That's not surprising, really, as our sense of smell is incredibly important to us, even before we're born. Of all the senses, it's the one that's most developed in the womb – and newborn babies have an unbelievably keen sense of smell. Within the first days of life they show a preference for the smell of their own mother, even before they can see her very clearly. Smell is the most developed sense in young children up until about the age of 10 when sight takes over.

For me, whenever I smell horses, saddle leather or hay, I am moved in a really profound way. When I visited my parents not long ago, my mother had to pick up some chicken feed from a livestock supplier. The overwhelming memory of all those childhood scents literally stopped me in my tracks. I sat on the floor and told my mother that I just really needed to sit there for a while. I sat for 30 minutes, thinking about my childhood on the back of my favourite horse and childhood companion, Bobby. The universe of scent inside that dusty shed, hay, leather and grain exposed a hidden reality some 30 years ago in a second. I'd found a time machine.

'What is essential is invisible to the eye,' Antoine de Saint-Exupéry wrote in his timeless children's book, *The Little Prince*. And in his wisdom, we must consider sound in these perfect worlds we are creating around us. It is almost as if this lost sense in a space, when it is found, becomes exponentially more powerful.

138

TULIP AND WILLOW (1875)

William Morris championed the handmade, skilled craftsmanship and the natural during an era that pushed relentlessly for industrial progress. When he was 16, he went with his parents to the the Great Exhibition, which was held in London's Hyde Park and focused on Machine Age design. The story goes that he rushed out as soon as he saw its contents, which he described as 'wonderfully ugly'.

139

WILD TULIP (1884)

William Morris wallpaper and fabric designs, based on English gardens and the natural world, are still popular around the world today. He was a key figure in the Arts and Crafts movement in England and helped revolutionise Victorian taste. It's inspiring to know that one person with such strong beliefs and a commitment to design can have such an ongoing influence on the way our homes look.

Music laps directly at our souls, like the sea on a shore. It has such a profound and immediate emotional and spiritual power over us. I can turn any bland hotel room in the world into a sanctuary purely by putting on some music; I can turn a car into a concert or a busy cafe into a cathedral with the right pair of noise cancelling headphones and choral music. We are a music-making species, even if we can't play any instruments ourselves.

Iégor Reznikoff, from the University of Paris-Nanterre, has shown that, most often, Stone Age art is found in the parts of caves where sound lingers or reverberates the most. Flutes of bone are often found nearby and red markings on walls lead to difficult-to-find acoustically perfect spots. Even in early life, our cave homes were filled with art, ritual and song. It's fundamental to who we are, and it's the fastest way to transform any space around you.

Finally, this leads us to consider taste. Food provides us with sustenance, but it is also the social glue which brings us together. It's the centre of celebrations, the signal of the season we are in and it shapes our days, as we organise all other activities around breakfast, lunch and dinner. Above all the other senses, taste is used to show our love for each other, the core of our most meaningful moments together, from our mother's milk to falling in lust over a first date dinner.

By considering all the five senses in your spaces, a wholeness emerges. A constellation of wonder and delight shaped just for you of memory, imagination, celebration and occasion. Our senses are our tools to explore our worlds, and it's through them that we can create our realities.

FAMILY FOUNDED, GEELONG, AUSTRALIA

I feel lucky enough to know the owner of this dear home – she's a student of mine. Initially exploring the possibility of hosting a home, Sharon has found her true passion in delighting the senses of others in ways that delight her. She now has a home store which also holds workshops. She collects and restores, teaches, photographs and includes her family in her work as much as possible.

142

EXPERIMENT 1:

When life inside our spaces depends on our objects, it helps to think beyond
aesthetics. Experiment one is beautiful, yes. But do you feel a sense of belonging
and purpose at this table?

143

EXPERIMENT 2:

At this table, I have an instinct to dwell, converse, enjoy. Visual beauty is important,
but equally so too are our other senses. Consider the balance of senses in style
and spaces rather than favouring aesthetic superiority.

144

STERREKOPJE, FRANSCHHOEK MOUNTAINS, SOUTH AFRICA

Fleur and Nicole of Sterrekopje, a healing farm, recognise the need to nurture all the senses and emotional needs of their guests, rather than just provide a place to stay. Each element has been carefully chosen by them to foster deep rest and reflection. Even an item as utilitarian as a basin can have impact – the sight and feel of it would make the simple act of washing a memorable experience.

145

STERREKOPJE, FRANSCHHOEK MOUNTAINS, SOUTH AFRICA

Above & pages 146–47 Stay, rest, grow and play are the cornerstones of Fleur and Nicole's approach to looking after visitors, and you can sense this intention in all their choices, including the way they put together places for bathing and lounging. The smooth timber of the chair against the woven wallcovering; the stone of the bath contrasted with the cane chaise.

148

STERREKOPJE, FRANSCHHOEK MOUNTAINS, SOUTH AFRICA

Central to life at Sterrekopje is cooking and eating. At sunrise every morning, seasonal produce for the day's meals is harvested from the gardens, while other local artisans and growers contribute what is not grown on site. Fleur and Nicole's innate ability to nurture each of their guests' five senses has led to Sterrekopje being known for the rare and special experience it offers.

149

STERREKOPJE, FRANSCHHOEK MOUNTAINS, SOUTH AFRICA

Even without being in this room, you know how it would make you feel. The warmth of the fire, the sound of it crackling, the scent of its burning wood. The feel of the kilim under your hand as you sit in the armchair. The sight of those oversized vegetables, so exuberant they make me want to smile. A pot of tea surely just out of frame. A room of one's own, elements to nurture the body and soul.

150

ALEX LEGENDRE, WEST SUSSEX, ENGLAND

Above & opposite Alex Legendre, joint founder of lifestyle shop and café I Gigi General Store, rescued this Edwardian house without erasing signs of its history. She loved its faded elegance, its peeling wallpaper and flaking paint, childhood drawings on the wall, and set about making a feature of them. The whole house is such an appeal to the senses – seeming imperfections only engage them more.

LA GRANDE OURSE, GLEN SPEY, USA

Pages 152–53 Juliette Hermant, a designer, an Antiquarian and a true favourite of mine when it comes to injecting senses and emotion into spaces, remodelled this '70s concrete block structure into an off-grid cabin in the woods in upstate New York. She has designed it to reconnect with the extensive history of the area and its very close relationship with nature.

156

APARTMENT, OSLO, NORWAY

Pages 154–55 Homes are machines that help us live well. The world outside our doors is so much out of our control, which is why it's important to attend to each of our senses in our own spaces rather than just concentrate on aesthetics. In this Oslo kitchen, comfortable as well as functional, all our senses would be engaged, to varying degrees, through the use of a range of materials and surfaces.

157

TWISS STREET, TASMANIA, AUSTRALIA

Opposite & above, pages 158–61 Christine, a warm and generous person, cares deeply about her house and the guests who stay there. A curator, she spends time in Sweden learning about traditional paint and finish techniques. She joined my school, The Hosting Masterclass, when she purchased this rundown property. While teaching her, she has also been teaching me about looking after old houses.

PART TWO

4
Places

Now that you have had a chance to explore the five lessons, I'd like to take you inside some of my favourite places ever and show you how those lessons can be used. I've searched around the world to find them – they're places that are honest and authentic, original and beautiful. To me, they say, more than anything, so much about the people who have put them together with such love and conviction.

One

SABI, TASMANIA, AUSTRALIA

I'm going to tell you a tale of what can happen when you allow yourself to be open to ideas and are willing to change your way of thinking; when – even though you've started down one path – you turn around and head in a different direction altogether.

This is the story of Jessica Eggleston, who had moved to Tasmania from Melbourne with her husband Fred and their two young children just a few months before she became a student of mine. Jessica and Fred had fallen in love with a cottage at Binalong Bay on the Bay of Fires and bought it immediately, even before they'd managed to buy their main family home. They did their sums to make sure they could afford it, but even so, it was an unexpected move for the couple. The cottage affected them in a way that was difficult to explain. It had been on the market for more than two years, which was surprising in such a sought-after part of the world, but not so surprising when you saw what the house used to look like. Jessica said it reminded her of a 1980s sauna, not in a good way, with its orange timber boards everywhere. And it had great thick stone walls, more the kind of place you'd find in the highlands. The fact that it seemed so out of place made Jessica and Fred love it more.

I met Jessica when she enrolled in my Hosting Masterclass. To make their buy work, they were going to need to let it out as a holiday rental, and she wasn't quite sure how to go about that, besides of course, ripping up the carpets, painting everything white and giving it a nautical feel.

I visited Jessica on site, and while walking around, letting her point out her plans to standardise this place in line with everything that surrounded it, I asked her if she wanted to hear my thoughts.

What I love about Jessica is that while she has very strong ideas, she's always open to new ones and, as I found out, is prepared to go somewhere she'd never imagined going.

When I looked at this place, it was the house itself that inspired me. Not what was currently working as holiday rentals in the area. All that wood and stone. All of its perfect imperfections, its odd proportions, everything so clumsily handmade it was incredibly charming. I showed her a few spaces that clung to the principles of wabi-sabi design that had always captured me, in the hope that she might be charmed by them too. What I wanted her to see is that her house was so utterly perfect and a work of art in itself; it just needed to be celebrated – not hidden.

Steering her away from white paint and encouraging her to work with what she had, I explained the basics of wabi-sabi to her; its principles of asymmetry, imperfection, incompleteness and impermanence are opposite to all that she'd ever been or known. She went home and did her research – she's very analytical and detail-focused in her professional life – and came up with the parts of wabi-sabi that resonated with her.

I'm so unbelievably proud of the work Jessica and Fred have done on their cottage, which is now called Sabi. When she and I were sitting in a little café in Binalong Bay, a spot on one of the tables was, to me, the exact walnut-y colour I could imagine the timber inside. She loved the idea so much that she and Fred added even more timber to the interior, and Jessica spent the next year staining every single board herself. That slow, methodical way of doing things fits with the idea of wabi-sabi, and she says she knows every board and every corner of the house so well that she has a different relationship with it than she could have thought possible.

Being in Tasmania has changed Jessica's way of thinking about things, she says. If she had been looking for a sofa in Melbourne, she would have jumped in the car and gone to five showrooms. That's not possible now, plus the cost of freight is enormous, so she and Fred have become creative and resourceful. She designed the sofas, and she and Fred made them, and the same goes for the platform beds. She looked for a dining table, but they were all too new and shiny, so she designed one herself and found a local carpenter to make it out of the most beaten-up reclaimed Tasmanian oak he had. He made the dining stools to her design as well. A local cooper made the bath for her from an old cider barrel; it's lined with salvaged copper fabricated by a sheet metal worker.

I love it that even though there are literally thousands of taps available, Jessica didn't think any of them were right, so she designed her own and had one of the old institutions in the closest big town, Launceston, make them up for her. The word 'bespoke' doesn't sound right for what Jessica and Fred have done – it seems more authentic and collaborative to be working with local tradespeople and artisans to create, over time, such special and individual objects throughout their house. There's something beautiful, she says, about getting to know those people, and witnessing the pride they have in their work. And it's made her feel more settled, more part of the community, in her new island home.

Discovering wabi-sabi – and I think, even more so, discovering this house and everything they have painstakingly created in it – has altered the way Jessica looks at the world as a whole, how she's planning to approach their family home, and even how she views herself. She never would have thought she would feel content with asymmetry or imperfection.

It is an honour to showcase what Jess and Fred have achieved. My schools provide an organised framework and support for our students to bring out the best in themselves and their spaces, but the hard work, creative ideas, ingenuity and tenacity belongs to them. Even before opening its doors to guests, Sabi had made its stamp on Tasmania and inspired many others. It is a testament to everything we stand for – authenticity, timelessness, togetherness and celebrating the incredible work our students create, far beyond what they ever dreamt they were capable of.

168

Above & opposite Bathing has become an important centrepiece of Sabi and of holidaying in Tasmania. Soaking and steaming after cold ocean plunges, or long walks in the mist, balance the nervous system in a way our counterparts in the Northern Hemisphere championed. Jess has taken it incredibly seriously, even designing her own taps as she couldn't find ready-made ones that were suitable.

Pages 170–75 Enjoying staying at Sabi for the first time after my first site visit there, I couldn't help but wonder at the painstaking work Jess and her family had lovingly applied to each stone, each board and every perfectly imperfect detail. You can feel that care and attention throughout. Where not restored by her hand, items have been made by local artisans and craftspeople.

Two

SORAYA AND MICHAEL
FORSBERG'S HOUSE, UMEÅ, SWEDEN

I love old houses. I'd rescue every one from being torn down or straightened up if I could. There's something about touching a wall that has seen so much more of life than you, which puts your place in this world into perspective. We are tactile and emotional beings, interacting with the stories of those who have come before us – and how time shapes a space ignites our senses and our humanness.

Soraya and Michael Forsberg's house, outside Umeå, way up in the north of Sweden, is such a beautiful example of how to celebrate and care for our ageing buildings while leaving their mark and writing their own chapter in it, too. I wanted to include it, dear reader, so that if you also share my love for these spaces you might be inspired by ageing buildings of your own.

This beautiful farmhouse is the home of the creative couple, their six children and two dogs. I know it looks like they have lived here forever, but actually they've only been there for a few years – having recently renovated the traditional old farmhouse, but in a way that speaks of layers and light, imperfection and story and of course, heritage.

It's plain to see in the mismatched doors, the stable doors, the decision to paint some things and not others. It's obvious, too, in the kitchen – I look in there and think of Goldilocks. The chairs of different sizes, colours and styles around the old wooden table, all a bit knocked about and collected along the way, I imagine, and one just right for each member of the family. A table this big with so many chairs around it would look overwhelming, and honestly a little bit boring, if everything matched – as it is,

it looks so cheerful and full of life and, even when no one's there, it's not difficult to imagine this delightful room being full of people. A really beautiful example like this can give you confidence to look around you and see what you've already got – it's so much nicer and more authentic to use things that have a bit of story to them. It also means that objects, loved for various reasons, can find their place. A plate of your grandmother's might not be something you'd want a whole set of, but could look lovely mixed in with other finds, and make you feel very happy when you use it.

Light is so important to Scandinavian design, mainly because there is so little of it for so much of the year. Out in the woods, there's no great need to use curtains on most of the windows – and where there are any, they're filmy enough to let in every little bit of light and hung in such a way that underlines just how relaxed this house is. Lamps sit on the floor, hang low over shelves or run on slack wire down a wall. The colours of walls, of ceilings, of floors, of fabrics, of objects are chosen to exude light in subtle ways, but not so perfect that they don't create shadows as well. There's a chalkiness, a roughness, a celebration of the mismatched timber wall boards. Whenever I'm putting together a room and think it's just about finished, I do the eyelash test on it, which involves squinting to see if any colours or textures are leaping out and looking out of place. I'm often surprised by what does jump out, but the space will look so much better without it. I'd do that test in any of the rooms in this house and there would be nothing to remove – it looks completely perfect as it is.

I love it that the house isn't too jam-packed – there's something so extravagant about leaving space in a room or on a landing to evolve or to be transformed on a daily basis.

Nothing looks too precious in this house – objects are placed on plinths, but then they might contain dried flowers or a single branch. And the plinths have character – roughened and as beautiful as the objects sitting on them. Garden pots are grouped on a desk, in full view of the living room; shelves are arranged haphazardly, which only makes them look more interesting. Objects, too, are grouped on the floor, where you don't expect to find them – the surprising placement or hanging of artwork and other things can help you look at them more carefully and enjoy them in a different way.

Often the simplest things can give us the most joy – I can imagine the mass of white flowers in a glass vase was collected from hedgerows or a tree in the garden, their scent wafting through the house and reminding the family of the lovely part of the country they live in and being a symbol of long summer days.

This old house sings with utter delight with the family who are its current custodians in time. I wonder constantly about the stories it has seen, how it might be to visit it now, and, as the years pass, what it will witness in the future.

Opposite, pages 180–85 The patchwork of surfaces affected by time and use are so evident in this lovely house in Sweden. Milled timber lining boards, hand-cut timbers, plaster, lime. The collection is a work of art. Nothing is too precious here, or too neatly arranged; everything has character, life and purpose. A ballet telling the story of this home and its occupants.

Syssla	Jämna Veckon	Udda Veckon
Plocka disk	James	Noel
Duka av	Benjamin Noel	James
Vika tvätt	Jack	James
Gå med sopor	Noel Benjamin	Benjamin
Tvätta t.tvätta tvätt	James	Noel
Klippa gräs/klippa (Trägårdsarbete)		Jack
Hämta på dans/bomal		Jack
Städa köket Badrum	James	Jack
Städa hallen WC&Vrum	Jack Noel Benjamin	Jack James Noel Benjamin
Dammsuga övervåning	Noel	James
Dammsuga nedervåning	Jack	Noel
Laga middag/lunch	Jack	

Skafferi

Three

FACTORIA VII, ADELAIDE HILLS, AUSTRALIA

I've adored this space for many years, coming across it after following its owners' store, Poet's Ode in the Adelaide Hills, which stocked the most delightful things. Handcrafted ceramics, a cushion cover dyed with plant-based dyes, an amazing scent, a vintage oil painting. Everything was simply displayed on old tables or cabinets, and classes, often by local makers, and exhibitions were held in a big room out the back. There was such a calm yet quietly thrilling feeling about Poet's Ode; it was created with such conviction for the simple, beautiful and rare things, and I always got the sense that they got as much out of their finds as all their customers did.

That sense of calm and conviction carries through to the house they lived in in a village in the Hills. It was built in the 1870s as a bacon factory (who knew such a thing existed!), and while anyone else might have been tempted to knock the industrial beginnings out of the building to turn it into a home, what I love about the approach to this space is its celebration of simplicity.

Just letting a beautiful thing be a beautiful thing. Sounds so basic, but it's rare to find in this world where everyone is eager to put their stamp on things and bring them into line with what everyone else is doing.

The balance between the house itself, and the family that lives inside is, to me, a symphony. The home's rough stone walls, its timber beams. Sitting perfectly besides what has been found, treasured, restored, curated, collected and foraged.

What I love, too, is that the owners have known when to stop with their own belongings and let the space continue with its own charm – the lintel above a door is left raw; the jarrah flooring has been stained a dark colour; the stoves and flues are black and utilitarian. And there's an industrial-style bench in the kitchen, inspired by the building's previous use as a factory.

The simple approach is refreshing – the vintage paintings, without frames, hanging on bulldog clips, curling at the edges. I think about how different this house would be if it were filled with perfection. Polished golden frames. Mirror-finished antiques, pin straight built-in modern kitchen.

Here, there's a story in every corner that makes me want to linger. The commitment to honesty follows through to the window coverings – fabric draped over a pole or pinned to rafters and knotted, or a painted shutter, shaped to follow the curve of the window. I can't tell you how happy it makes me just looking at such unadorned beauty.

Every now and then there's a surprise – the vintage sofa restored in deep blue velvet is unexpected, making it even more curious. Most furniture and bits and pieces had, at some point, been at Poet's Ode – I believe it's a good thing to use what you have, as much as possible. The owners had probably not expected to be living with pieces they had curated for the shop, and perhaps a blue velvet sofa may not have been their first choice, but it works brilliantly here.

I wanted to show you this home for its sense of conviction to celebrate what it is, what the owners treasure. I admire their sense of balance and restraint. The result is a home that will be forever beautiful. Forever a respite from all that is overwhelming about a fast paced, over-saturated life.

Four

HÔTEL PETER & PAUL, NEW ORLEANS, UNITED STATES

196

Spaces are machines that transport us instantly to how we'd like to feel, and it's to Hôtel Peter & Paul I'd like to go to step into utmost delight. Gingham, simple and humble, is used boldly here as the medium for instant happiness. There's something so dreamy and timeless about it, and instantly nostalgic. And it's not necessarily what you expect in a hotel found in what used to be a 19th-century school house, rectory, church and convent. The use of gingham in such a setting has made me fall in love with this place even more. And it's why, dear reader, I so desperately wanted to show you this magical hotel, to show you what is possible when you leave trend aside, and choose what charms you. What truly important and downright medicinal spaces you can create when you follow your bliss.

In a city with such a rich French heritage, the obvious choice would be to go for a French-inspired interior. And in religious buildings, it would have been easy to play that side up quite strongly. But that would have been instantly forgettable. Another themed hotel, built for profit not our pleasure. Like gingham itself, this interior is dreamy and timeless, confident and thoughtful. And completely whimsical in places. In the café with its rustic stools, walls have painted vines creeping around lampshades – do lemons really grow on vines (they do here and that's all that matters) – and a painted ceiling is striped like a circus tent, its painted fringed border edging over into cornices and architraves.

While it's beautiful and comfortable, with pretty well all its original features still intact, it's also unbelievably theatrical, in such a joyful way. I just want to be in the rectory lounge, where masses of mustard fabric have turned the room into a theatre set; gathered gingham, floor to ceiling, acts as a backdrop, with check shaded wall sconces set into it. And it has the most amazing collection of furniture you've ever seen. Nothing matches, but everything works perfectly – it's got the sort of look as if you've found stuff in antique shops or inherited it from a rich aunt with fantastic taste, and picked up other bits and bobs at garage sales and op shops. Delicate hand-painted furniture mixed with vintage cane chairs and an over-the-top table. A two-seater sofa that looks as if it came out of a French château, walls painted in chalky paint, ginghams mixed with florals.

Elsewhere, gilded mirrors sit alongside slightly bashed-up rush-seated chairs; a chandelier hangs over a bathtub. Timber tables with chairs could have come from a Wes Anderson movie; wardrobe doors have been painted in trompe l'oeil designs.

I always think if you're going to do something, you need to do it with a huge degree of certainty and sincerity, which the owner of this hotel has done.

It's not just in the surprising choices made, but also in the layers of beautiful elements, all working together. The tented reception desk inspired by Venetian and Indian palaces; room colours taken from iconic religious paintings. And that any changes to the buildings have been made sensitively – they're virtually the same outside as they always have been, which only makes what's happening inside even more wonderful.

Simply put, Hôtel Peter & Paul is a masterclass in creating spaces that buck trends and bring unabashed joy. I will be checking in at every opportunity.

197

202

Pages 198–201, above & opposite In a city like New Orleans, it would be so easy to play up its strong French history. Instead, the approach is far more playful, but carefully considered. Gingham in multiple sizes makes an appearance in guest rooms; there's a circus tent feel to the café and a touch of whimsy. There's a focus on the unexpected here, and that's always to be celebrated.

203

Pages 204–11 Combining opulence and simplicity is not the easiest thing to do, but it's done so confidently here. Why it works so well is that along with the opulence there's restraint, and the simplicity is carried out with humour and conviction. In less skilled hands, it would be easy to feel overwhelmed or even confused by the spaces; here, they hang together perfectly.

PART THREE

10
Rooms

I see hundreds of rooms a year, and each time I do, I ask myself the very simple question, 'Is this somewhere you want to be?' Often the answer is yes, but then I'll wonder how *long* I actually want to spend there. With the 10 rooms I'm taking you to here, I could happily stay for days, months, forever. These are rooms I keep going back to – each one demonstrates the lessons we've covered in this book. I'll explain how, and also let you explore them on your own.

THE BUSHKILL HOUSE

Pennsylvania, United States

For a cabin in the woods, this couldn't be a more perfect kitchen, which is not really surprising. When Lauren Lochry and Jeff Gillway of the Brooklyn, New York, design studio Ridge House are creating a space, they always think about story first of all – whether it's what life used to be like when a house was first built or, in the case of this little place in the Pocono Mountains, what's going on in the surrounding area. It's such an inspiring way to start thinking about what a space might be, not what it is supposed to be. The couple is also always checking out garage sales and looking into skips to see what they can work with. It means their rooms, even if they're only just finished, always look as if they've evolved over time. The timber of the cabinets, ceiling and furniture echo the surrounding woods; the room is beautifully shadowy, with glimpses of light which, again, feels like an extension of what's happening outside. Notice how the glasses in the cabinet and the drawer handles are subtle bright spots in the room – as I've mentioned before, light doesn't necessarily come from completely obvious sources. It would be tempting in a room like this to overfill it – I love the way Lauren and Jeff have included just a few carefully chosen objects, including the lovely pieces hanging above the cooktop and the artwork propped up on the counter top. I pore longingly over this beautiful kitchen.

GIL BONGIORNO'S HOUSE

Pavia, Italy

There's such a sense of intentional calm in the whole of this beautiful house in Pavia. Before becoming a manor in around 1400, it was a convent and was considered a place of worship for the Knights Templar. Part of its calm comes from there being a deliberately unfinished quality to it – almost like a story partly told, giving you the chance to write the next chapter. With magnificent spaces that sing sweetly enough as they are, why would you want to do any more than is needed to live well.

Wonder also plays its part here, in its mix of traditional and quite grand furniture with contemporary artwork, in its minimal approach to decoration – with polished concrete flooring there's not a rug in sight – and, in this room, with its unusual lighting solution. Why settle for one lamp? Enjoy the things you love, curate your light perfectly for your every desire throughout the day. The artwork here is so bold, so extraordinary and, yes, so large, that the room needs nothing else – the owner has achieved a real sense of balance, understanding that anything more could have been overwhelming, or overwhelmed. This room speaks to me about the beauty of solitude, the sense of a hermitage which I have always so strongly desired, and space to breathe and imagine, letting ideas appear and distractions disappear.

THE DORA MAAR HOUSE

Ménerbes, France

What is it about the French – they seem to intrinsically understand what works as far as colour and texture go. I'm convinced they are all born with great taste. Occasionally I find myself browsing real estate adverts in the small southern farming town where I have found myself in autumn for many years now, and even the most rudimentary of bachelor pads seem put together with the taste and grace of the world's most skilled.

In all my work, I strive to find and showcase humble spaces, along with the grand – and the perfectly loved and designed. Beauty is not a product of budget or experts, it's a product of whoever lives in the space. It's about being authentic.

In this sitting room you'll find wool against brick; kilim with linen. There's the sense that if you love something, there's a magic that makes it work. And I love the way they go about collecting and curating – in the case of this lovely room in southern France, it's all to do with building a space that's just right for the people using it, rather than creating a space for others to look at and admire. It's essentially about comfort, about having meaningful things around, and close at hand, and not too perfectly straight. Those gorgeous cabinets of books look far more inviting to me because they're slightly higgledy-piggledy – I'm sure they'd be full of treasures. It's about having couches you love – and it's much better if they don't match, bonus points if they were gifted by a family member or a neighbour – and lamps in the right spot. And rugs that looked as if they've lived other lives and curtains that have seen other windows. It could be tempting to clean the fireplace up, but then it would lose its history – remnants of smoke from hundreds of winters just add to the beauty of this room. Perfection in imperfection, in you, its custodian.

REVERS DE FORTUNE

Ardèche, France

Valérie Rambaud and Sébastian Verger, who live in the Ardèche in southeastern France, are true creatives – curious and restless, imaginative and always with a unique take on the world. He's been passionate about archaeology since he was a little boy; she's into writing stories and poetry. A couple I would dearly love to knock on the door of one day – I'm sure they have some tales to tell! They've been collaborating for decades on so many different things, including antiques and interior decoration, jewellery making and fashion. When I look at their kitchen, their story is so close at hand – this is a place to collaborate, to enjoy being in, and it's a place in which loved objects and varying collections are far more prominent than utensils and other practical bits and pieces. It's a space in which the curve is dominant – the animal horns, the mask, the wooden pieces hanging. So, too, is the humble but fail-safe triangle method of arranging objects – they may not be obvious, but look carefully and you can find several triangles among the objects. It's why some arrangements work, and others – whose residents have yet to be taught the triangle trick – don't. This glorious kitchen for these two creatives is full of textures and layers, wonder and delight – smooth and shiny pieces hanging on the rough timber wall; the curtain instead of cupboard doors. I love its limited palette and its element of surprise; more than anything, I love the fact that this couple have made a kitchen that suits them – they don't need anyone to tell them what a kitchen should look like. What a joy it would be to be in this space; I might even start to enjoy cooking – or if I get invited for dinner, sit blissfully in this kitchen and let a magical night of conversation unfold.

MARINA RENDLE'S HOUSE

Hay-on-Wye, United Kingdom

When I talk about a space being the expression of one's own personal universe and cosmos, this is what I mean. This living room is like walking into a Vermeer painting – one in which such beauty is found in its light and shadow; and in the fact that everything looks well loved and well worn in the most perfect way. Van Gogh, in a letter to his brother, wrote that 'life is probably round'. It's something that's always stuck with me, and a question that I'm always pondering. Currently I think the answer is 'likely'. All life starts as an egg.

When I look through the doorway into this room, I can't help thinking about how secure we feel when using rounds in our spaces – there is no greater form that affects how we feel. It is there in the mirror over the fireplace; the shell hanging on the wall; the vessels massed on top of the cabinet. It's there, too, in the arms and back of the sofa, the design of the rug, the wall sconces over the mantelpiece, the hoops. In the world of design education and commentary, there are plenty of instances of a 'quick fix', '10 tips', or 'how to style your shelf', but they don't actually help us to mimic what others have done. I think they cause more pain than pleasure, but I am often asked what quick tips I can give. There are no shortcuts, as my students have discovered at my schools; I can't teach you everything in one breath, conversation or book. But I do often say the secret to making any space feel pleasurable to be in, no matter your aesthetic, is by using more rounded edges than straight. It is genuinely the only quick fix I know!

PALAZZO DANIELE

Gagliano del Capo, Italy

Let me show you my favorite bathroom of all time – why shouldn't bathing be a grand experience? When you exaggerate anything – spaces included – it sparks a sense of wonder. Housed in an aristocratic palazzo in the south of Italy, the bathroom speaks to the importance of the curve, and definitely passes what I call the eyelash test, in which when I squint and look at a space, nothing jars. It also shows that grand doesn't necessarily mean opulent; I love it that everything is on display and that there's no more here than is absolutely necessary – the old-fashioned radiator looks perfectly appropriate, and so, too, do the simple towel and clothes hooks. Wouldn't it be amazing to have a shower in this room – what an ingenious and beautiful set-up, made even more wonderful by the fact that there's no attempt at all to hide the plumbing pipes. Light and shadow play such an important role in this space. The dappled shaft of light coming into the room; the way light and shadow manage to transform even everyday objects and fittings, such as the towels and radiator; the play of light on the shower in the centre of the room.

SARAH AND ADAM HALL'S PLACE

Willunga, Australia

Sarah's a student of mine and, after doing one of my classes, set about carefully turning this old church in the McLaren Vale, South Australia, into a family home. There's a real sense of play here, and an exploration of form and design. I really admire the way she's been experimenting and finding her way as the renovation has progressed – there have been so many tests with different natural paints, and she's been playing around with thrift shop finds to make sure they're in just the right spot. She's embraced the circle in all its many forms, and has found balance in not trying to cram too much into the space – it could have been tempting to add one extra element to the wall to the left of the doorway. This room is her space for calm in family life. I especially love the strange proportions as the top of the doorway is cut off – it really is my favourite part of the room. There is charm in imperfection, and there is genius when it is intentional to make a room one's own. Perhaps it's because we're all so delightfully imperfect that it's only natural that our rooms should follow suit.

Sarah and her sister Emma have gone on to do great things after attending my class. Over the past few years they have created two wildly different beach cottages as holiday rentals – they're exploring their own design voices, and have been so incredibly successful that they've been able to quit their day jobs. They have launched an online shop selling curated finds that they love, and have built such a wonderful following of their own, becoming an inspiration to so many.

ROOM 8

FRÉDÉRIQUE MORREL'S APARTMENT

Paris, France

Frédérique Morrel is an artist whose Paris apartment is both a home and studio. She works with old tapestries and taxidermy moulds to create fantastical creatures that look as if they've stepped straight out of the pages of a fairytale; her creations have been found in all sorts of places, including the windows of Hermès on Madison Avenue in New York. Having seen her art, it's so obvious to me that her bedroom would not only be unconventional, but so truly individual and unmistakably hers. The unfinished walls; the lightbox bedside table with nothing practical on it; the unmatched sheets; the chalky textures that provide such a contrast to her own colourful artwork. Like a bowerbird, she has very carefully curated collections. And like a bowerbird, she wants to be surrounded by her collections. We often think of our bedrooms as nests – spaces in which we gather bits and pieces that we deeply love and that nurture us. Most of us have at least a little bit of bowerbird in us – I know I do – and Frédérique's space eggs me on to keep piling high around me what I hold so authentically dear.

CASA SILVIA ANGELI

Milan, Italy

I've always wondered why kitchens follow such a bland formula instead of being treated with the same personal and individual attention as bedrooms and living rooms. They're usually designed so they look a bit like domestic laboratories, with no permission to put your own stamp on them. The 'kitchen triangle', a decades-old formula for arranging your sink, stove and refrigerator, suggests that the distance between each should be between about one- and two-and-a-half metres, and the sum of all three sides of the triangle should be between about four and eight metres. While it isn't always appropriate for every situation, it's a good place to start in terms of functionality, but the attention to the design of the space usually ends with that – apart from displaying a few bits and pieces around the place. That's why I love this kitchen so much – it really explores the idea of a kitchen. It's so much more than a space to cook in – it's a space to curate, to live in, to spend time in. And more than that, it's so much part of the entire home – no concessions are made for the fact that it's partly a functional space. Lavish potted plants, a fireplace, hanging sculptures, candelabras – not necessarily what you expect to see in a kitchen, but so much the better for it.

MY PLACE

I've always been challenged by bright, symmetrical, linear, flat, bulk-built Western homes, which have always felt primitive to me. I prefer the shadowy, curious, monastic spaces made by those who see homes as an artform to help our daily lives. I still remember the first space I ever became intrigued with, a small hermitage in Geraldton, Western Australia, built by Monsignor John Hawes, a priest, architect and self-described artist and hermit. A small, dark, oddly proportioned space for one, designed to simply reflect in for a period of weeks or months. It was built to be his retirement home. An inscription on the ceiling in Latin 'Remite mihi ut refrigerer priusquam abeam et amplius non ero' roughly translates to 'O spare me, that I may recover my strength, Before I go hence and be no more.'

I became obsessed with having a hermitage of my own one day, and if I couldn't have this one which I loved and longed for so dearly as a child, I was determined to find my own. And I did. If you Google Monsignor Hawes and his work on The Hermitage, it is almost an exact match for the one I have found here in Tasmania. The similarities between the two buildings has firmly cemented my belief that perhaps all our birthday wishes do one day come true.

I spend more time in this room than any other. Its curves make me feel held and human. I'm careful to not have more than I need here. A chair in front of the fire, and a couch looking out to the water. A small cooker. A bed upstairs surrounded by books. My hermitage waits silently for me, in a forest on the sea. Its night lights are like stars, waiting to help me navigate my way home, so that I may recover my own strength, before I go hence and be no more.

FINAL THOUGHTS

Life so far has taught me that we are infinitely more powerful, and infinitely less important than I once thought we were. When I think about what we are – star-dusted faraway atoms of consciousness – and how vast and complex this universe we live in is, I shrug my shoulders and ask myself, 'What does it really matter anyway?'. But then I think about our universe within. Our complex bodies designed as machines of emotions, hard-wired to render our entire experience of our times on Earth. And know that the opportunity we have been gifted is to create our own realities, whatever they may be, that bring us pleasure, joy, security, love, without too much care for what anyone else thinks.

A couple of years ago, I had gone out for a solitary evening row after the sun had set on the dark and mysterious body of water – where it is said that ancient sea monsters still exist – that lies out the front of my cabin, Captains Rest. A few hundred metres from shore, the surface of the water was so still that you could no longer make out the horizon. The stars above reflecting on the inky water appear as a single sphere of a galaxy, inside which I was floating. It was out there, thinking about the students I was currently in session teaching – cautiously sharing their own gut-wrenching tales of woe that life brings, enthusiastically exchanging memories, objects and ideas which bring them true joy: Australian bush poetry, the sunny '80s shack yellow, a window seat with a book in reach – that I realised for the first time that we are all just little ships drifting along a starry sea on our way to faraway ports we are yet to know much about, and no one's journey is without peril.

My work is about giving those who wish for them the tools to build magical worlds of their own and the wholehearted encouragement to do so. Five elements of style to consider in our spaces to create poetry around us. Of all the journeys I have been on, it is sharing this one with all of you, as you navigate your own uncharted waters and wash ashore somewhere heavenly, which has become the greatest.

PLACES

The Bowmont
thebowmont.com.au
@thebowmont

Captains Rest
captainsrest.com
@captainsrest

Château de la Carrière
ourfrenchcountrychateau.com
@ourfrenchcountrychateau

The Cold Press
thecoldpress.com
@the_cold_press

Hôtel Peter and Paul
ash.world/hotels/peter-and-paul
@hotelpeterandpaul

The Landscape Lodge
thelandscapelodge.com
@thelandscapelodge

Marston House
marstonhouse.com
@marstonhouse

Novecento
novecento.biz

Palazzo Daniele
palazzodaniele.com
@palazzo.daniele

Sabi
sabistays.com
@sabi.stays

Sterrekopje
sterrekopje.com
@sterrekopjefarm

Twiss Street
@twissstreet

PEOPLE

AP Design House
apdesignhouse.com.au
@apdesignhouse
Pages 78–83, 112–15

Atelier Ellis
atelierellis.co.uk
@atelier.ellis
Page 119

Atelier Vime
ateliervime.com/en/
@ateliervime
Pages 19–24

Rachel Baker
www.3sources.com
@3_sources
Pages 92, 93

Monique Fedor
moniquefedor.com
@moniquefedor_
Pages 71, 105

Family Founded
familyfounded.com.au
@family_founded
Page 141

Val Harris
thetablehay.com
@thetablehay
Pages 130–35

Alastair Hendy
aghendy.com
@alastairhendy
Pages 54–57

Juliette Hermant
maisonbergogne.com
@maisonbergogne
Pages 152, 153

Sarah Nedovic
sarahnedovic.com
@sarahnedovicgaunt
Page 252

Kirsten Perry
kirstenperry.com
kirstenpp
Page 44

Predrag Pajdic
treasurecabinet.com
@predrag_pajdic
Pages 120, 121

Read & Hall
readandhall.com.au
@readandhall
Pages 18, 231–33

Retrouvius
retrouvius.com
@retrouvius
Pages 46–49

Ridge House
www.ridgehouse.co
@_ridgehouse
Pages 215–17

Lucy Rollef
lucyroleff.com
@lucyroleff
Page 104

Dakota Yewen
@dakotayewen
Page 252

Every reasonable effort has been made to acknowledge the copyright of images in this volume. Any errors or omissions that may have occurred are inadvertent, and will be corrected in subsequent editions provided notification is sent in writing to the publisher.

PHOTOGRAPHERS

Sarah Andrews
www.sarahandrews.co
@sarahandrews.co
Pages 108, 109, 110, 111

Sveinung Bråthen/
House of Pictures
sbraathen.no
Pages 13, 14–15

Peter Crosby
petercrosbyphotography.com
@pbcrosby
Pages 152, 153

Francesco Dolfo/Living Inside
francescodolfo.com
@francescodolfophotography
Pages 69, 72–73, 88, 89, 219

Rory Gardiner
rory-gardiner.com
@arorygardiner
Pages 78–83, 112–15

Marnie Hawson
marniehawson.com.au
@marniehawson
Pages 18, 141, 186, 188–95,
231, 232–33

Hotel Peter & Paul Press Images
(photo credit Courtesy of Hotel
Peter & Paul)
ash.world/hotels/peter-and-paul
@hotelpeterandpaul
Pages 196, 198–210

Alessandra Ianniello/
Living Inside
Pages 239–41

Emma Jude Jackson
emmajudejackson.com
@missemmajude
Page 145

Nathalie Krag/House of Pictures
@nathaliekragphotographer
Pages 96, 97

Kalina Krawczyk
kalinaphotography.co.uk
@kalina_krawczyk
Pages 118, 119

Kristian Septimius Krogh/
House of Pictures
septimiuskrogh.dk
@kristianseptimiuskrogh
Pages 50–53

Kim Lightbody
kimlightbody.com
@kim.lightbody_photography
Pages 46–49

Lauren Lochry
www.ridgehouse.co
@_ridgehouse
Pages 215, 216–17

Antonella Machet
slowlivinghideaway.com/en/
@slowlivinghideaway
Pages 30, 31, 60–63, 90, 91, 229

Joanna Maclennan
joannamaclennan.com
joannamaclennanphotography
Front cover and pages 19–24, 58,
92–95, 103, 106–07, 116, 117, 120,
121, 128–35, 154–55, 225, 226–27

Mark C. O'Flaherty/Living
Inside
markcoflaherty.com
@markc_oflaherty
Pages 74–77

Lina Östling/House of Pictures
linaostling.se
@fotograflinaostling
Pages 84–87, 176, 179–85

Michael Paul/Living Inside
michaelpaulphotography.co.uk
Pages 54–57, 150–51

Carole Poirot
carolepoirot.com

@carole.poirot
Page 25

Inge Prins
ingeprins.com
@inge_prins
Pages 144, 148, 149

Ruth Ribeaucourt
thefrenchmuse.com
@ruthreibeaucourt
Pages 32, 33, 122–27, 221,
223, 235, 236–37

Cassie Sullivan
cassiesullivan.com
@cassiesullivan_._
Pages x–xi, 29, 243–47, 255, 259

Christoph Theurer/House of
Pictures
@christophtheurer
Pages 26, 27, 28

Lean Timms
leantimms.com
@leantimms
Pages 39, 40–41, 59, 156–61,
164, 167–75

Jessica Tremp
jessicatremp.com
@jessicatremp
Back cover and pages ii, vi, 5, 8, 16,
17, 34, 42–45, 64, 70, 71, 98, 104,
105, 136, 142, 143, 252, 253, 257

Elsa Young
elsayoung.photography
@elsa47
Page 146

Raw Pixel/rawpixel.com
Images used under Creative
Commons license
Pages 10, 11, 36, 37, 66, 67, 100,
138, 139

ABOUT THE AUTHOR

Sarah Andrews, scientist and designer, is the bestselling author of *Principles of Style*, founder of The Hosting Masterclass, widely praised as the leading school in the world for designing and creating hosting homes, and designer of Captains Rest, which has become an icon. She has recently launched her new school, Principles of Styling & Storytelling, which is a school for everyone – and is busy working on her next property for everyone to enjoy, Far Away Farm.

Sarah was born and raised in Geraldton, Western Australia. She was a spatial scientist working in London before setting out to try to sail around the world on her own in her mid-twenties. A shock sinking on a dark and stormy night off the coast of Mexico nearly led to the loss of her life, after which she lived possessionless on a remote beach close to where she lost her boat, *Gabrielle*. The incident prompted a return to university in Melbourne to pursue her first passion, design.

Sarah has combined her background in sciences and art to bring process and formula to what was once subjective, dramatically changing the course of thousands of her students' lives. Her school started as three grass-roots community workshops – the success of so many of her students led her work to gain cult status, and has grown into an online school teaching globally.

Her work is about putting beauty back into the hands of those whom monoculture and elitism has pushed out. Dispelling the mystery and myths of the creative world and interior spaces, and ultimately advocating for all those who are looking for their own voice. Sarah officially lives in The Hermitage on the Sea, in Southern Tasmania but is rarely there, preferring to spend her life exploring the world almost constantly. She is especially interested in historical and faraway lesser known places, and would love you to reach out if you have a castle, island, boat or cabin she might be able to visit one day. If you are interested in joining one of her schools, or coming to stay in one of her properties, you can find her online at www.sarahandrews.co or on Instagram at @sarahandrews.co. She is always excited to meet a new friend online.

ACKNOWLEDGEMENTS

There should be a list of names on the cover of this book, not just mine. The talented and kind people responsible for you reading what you hold in your hands now are Leta Keens, who has the worst job ever of editing and writing my incoherent thoughts coherently. Chelsea and the team at Hardie Grant, who I am forever grateful to for their trust in me. Julie Gibbs, who I have always been a fan of, and met when she became a student of mine. Now she's my agent, and I'm still a fan. Evi O and her team, the most progressive book designers on Earth, but patient enough with me to lay things out how I'd like them to be. Amanda Starkey, who turned up early with chocolate-coated macadamias to my first class, and has never left my side through every book, class or property we have worked on. I always say that when you retire, so will I. I could do none of this without you. Or want to! And Tara, thank you for working on the small things so the big things can happen.

I also have to thank the rest of the incredible team involved in this book. Establishment Studios for your space, Jessica Tremp for your photos, Paige Anderson and Vivien Hollingsworth for helping with the experiments, Claire Leighton for always making me look my best and giving me a giggle, Emma-Jane Christie and Adele O'Shea for making my clothes. To all the photographers included in this book, I especially want to thank you for your images and your kindness in supplying them, and for supporting me. I do not take the honour of publishing your art lightly. To the owners of the properties featured – the book couldn't happen without you, so thank you for allowing us in.

To the team that make my books, my schools, my properties, my world turn. Cheryl Carr, Lisa McKernan, Jess, Mikaela, Tahlia and Bob Tresdale of Captains Rest, Kurt and Jan who take care of things while I'm away. Daniel, Steve, James, Jake and everyone hard at work on Far Away Farm, thank you, what an honour to work with you. I am forever indebted.

I'm one lucky human. Mimi Knoop, my partner. I love you more than yesterday – and after watching me at my worst, agonising over two books, I'm relieved you do too. Jordan Jones, Nick Jaffe, Benitha Vlok. Lifelong friendships I feel honoured to be a part of. The Andrews Family, Mum and Dad, Laura, Josh, Sarah, Joel, Sam, Olivia, Leo, Ivy, Max. If I could choose anyone to be loved by and related to, I would still choose you guys. What a bunch of unique, eccentric characters you are. You've all given me permission to do great, dangerous and funny things – which has gifted me the happiness I've now found in life.

And finally to my students. Past, present and future. It's only you who know what a truly magnificent journey we have all been a part of together. Thank you for trusting me.

257

'Not about what
a home should
be made of,
it's a guidebook
to what it is –
a shelter and an
incubator for our
unique humanness.'

Published in 2023 by Hardie Grant Books,
an imprint of Hardie Grant Publishing

Hardie Grant Books (London)
5th & 6th Floors
52–54 Southwark Street
London SE1 1UN

Hardie Grant Books (Melbourne)
Building 1, 658 Church Street
Richmond, Victoria 3121
hardiegrantbooks.com

British Library Cataloguing-in-Publication Data.
A catalogue record for this book
is available from the British Library.

The Poetry of Spaces
ISBN: 978-1-78488-658-5

1 3 5 7 9 10 8 6 4 2

Publishing Director: Kajal Mistry
Acting Publishing Director: Emma Hopkin
Senior Editor: Chelsea Edwards
Design: Evi O Studios
Commissioning Editor: Eve Marleau
Editor: Leta Keens
Proofreader: Marie Clayton
Senior Production Controller: Katie Jarvis

Colour reproduction by p2d
Printed and bound in China by
Leo Paper Products Ltd.